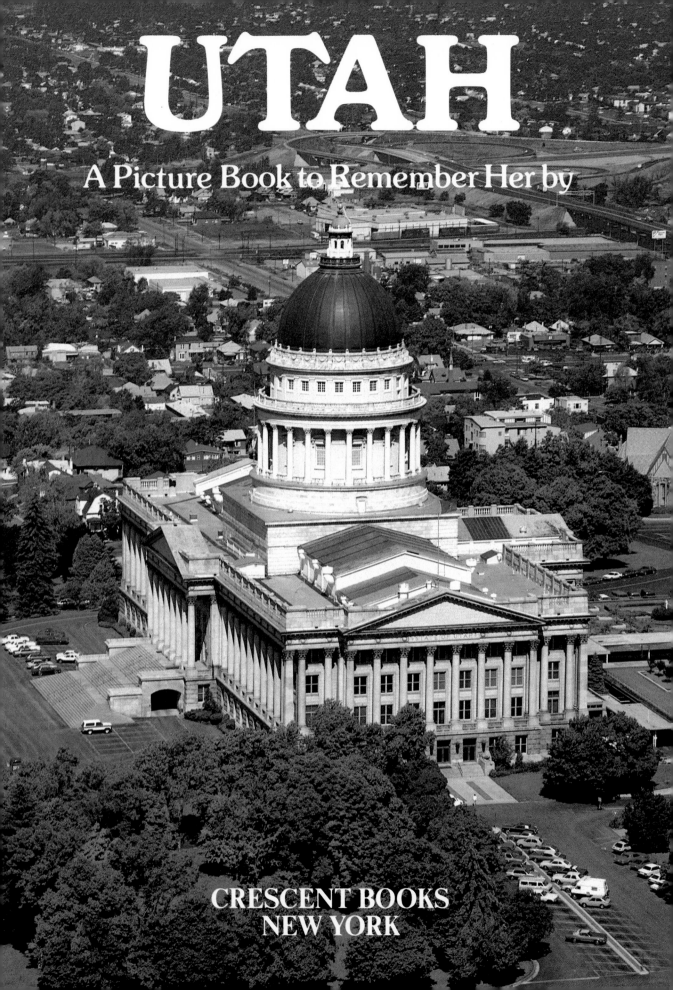

UTAH

A Picture Book to Remember Her by

CRESCENT BOOKS
NEW YORK

CLB 863
© 1985 Illustrations and text: Colour Library Books Ltd.,
    Guildford, Surrey, England.
Text filmsetting by Acesetters Ltd., Richmond, Surrey, England.
Printed in Spain.
Published 1985 by Crescent Books, distributed by Crown Publishers, Inc.
ISBN 0 517 478072
h g f e d c b a

Americans are proud to point out that their country was founded by people who wanted to escape religious persecution. But all too often, the founding fathers and their offspring practiced persecution themselves. Utah is a living monument to it.

The story began along New York State's Erie Canal in 1827, when a young man named Joseph Smith is said to have had a vision that led to the founding of a new religion known as the Church of Jesus Christ of Latter-day Saints, the Mormon Church.

His followers, driven from place to place, usually violently, finally, in 1847, trekked nearly 1400 miles from Illinois out onto the Great Plains until they reached a spot in the Western desert, stopping when their leader, Brigham Young, declared, "This is the place."

The place he chose to establish the "new Zion" was as hostile as the Negev itself, but the Mormons knew they could make the desert bloom. They were successful, of course, but it was never easy. By 1877, when Brigham Young died, there were 140,000 Mormons in more than 3250 communities working hard at the job.

Discrimination followed them west and their applications for statehood fell on deaf ears in Washington for another two decades before they joined the community of states.

About 75 percent of all Utahns are Mormons today, and the principles of their religion pervade every aspect of life from the state's economy to its government. They believe in hard work, a close-knit family and total abstinence, among other things. The result is that life in Utah isn't quite like life in the other Western states, where individualism is an article of faith. They have the highest birthrate of any state, one of the highest literacy rates and a disposition to stay put that makes its population one of the country's most stable. There is probably less smoking, less drinking, less card-playing done in Utah than any state, East or West.

Utahns are like other Westerners in one respect, their love of the land. Their grandfathers went through such hardship to claim it, the love is only natural. It's a place of desert stillness and mountain beauty. The irrigated greenbelt at the center in the shadow of the Washatch Mountains, the gray desert around the Great Salt Lake, the red and yellow desert in the east, the snow-capped mountains with their sparkling lakes and pine-covered plateaus, are all among the things they love. Until very recent years, the main tourist attraction in Utah was the desire to "see a Mormon." Except to visit the famous and beautiful Tabernacle on Mormon Square in Salt Lake City, the lure is different these days. People go there now to see the strangely beautiful countryside that inspired Brigham Young to say: "This is the place."

Queen's Garden Trail, in Bryce Canyon National Park.

Bottom left: rock formations, and (below) Squaw Flat, in the Needles district of Canyonlands National Park. Bottom center left: the Indian paintbrush, and (bottom center right) flowers of the western peppergrass. Bottom far right: peppergrass blooms in profusion below the Wooden Shoe. Soaring Double Arch (right) in Arches National Park, the heart of the famous red rock country of Utah.

Right: the Organ rock formation, and (below) the Garden of Eden, in Arches National Park. Bottom left: the road leading into Devil's Lane. Bottom right: figures dwarfed by rocks, seen from Big Spring Canyon Overlook, and (center right) sunset beyond Island in the Sky, both in Canyonlands National Park. Far right: the arid Flats, near Canyon Overlook, Canyonlands National Park.

Below and bottom center: views from the Grand View Point of Island in the Sky, Canyonlands National Park, show the vast scale of the red landscape carved by wind and rain, and by the Colorado River and its tributaries. Right: the orange sandstone of South Park Avenue, in Arches National Park. Bottom left: western peppergrass flourishes in the dry climate of the Colorado Plateau. Far right center: evening sunlight on the trail near Peekaboo Spring, and (far right bottom) the Needles area of Canyonlands National Park. Overleaf: the Needles, beyond the dry scrub of Chesler Park, Canyonlands National Park.

Far left: petroglyphs carved on Newspaper Rock by the Anasazi Indians, who hunted and farmed the land now designated as Canyonlands National Park from about AD 400 until approximately 1250. Left: a rough road, and (below far left) a deep, shadowed canyon carved by Salt Creek, both in the Needles district of Canyonlands National Park. Below left: the Devil's Kitchen, and (below right) Angel Arch, which stands over 190 feet high at the end of Salt Creek Trail. Bottom: the vast entrance to Joint Trail, leading to Chesler Park. Overleaf: silhouette of Delicate Arch, in Arches National Park.

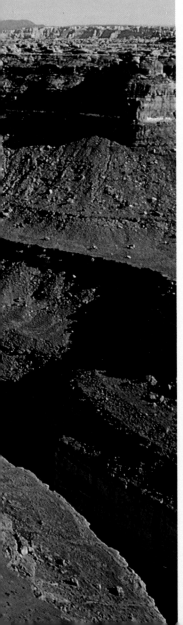

Arches National Park contains a concentrated assemblage of spectacular rock formations and colorings, including (far left) North Window, framing Turret Arch, and (below right) South Window. Left: the Devil's Garden and (below left) Upper Fiery Furnace, also in Arches National Park. Below far left: the North and South Six-shooter Peaks, Canyonlands National Park, and (bottom) the Needles district of Canyonlands, drained by Salt Creek. Overleaf: layers of colored rock, eroded by wind and water into the contrasting textures of the Castle, in Capitol Reef National Park. The spectacular coloring of Utah's scenery is due to the presence of iron oxides in the rock, mixed with varying concentrations of manganese and copper.

Top left: hard stone caps Chimney Rock, in Capitol
Reef National Park, where (top center and top right)
erosion has pitted and scored the rocks at Capitol
Gorge and (far right and overleaf) beyond the arch of
Hickman Natural Bridge. Above: Twin Rocks, and (right)
the Egyptian Temple, both in Capitol Reef National
Park. Above right: claret cup cactus.

Right: the old schoolhouse at Fruita. Bottom center right: Eph Hanks Tower, in Capitol Reef National Park. This park encompasses the Waterpocket Fold, which runs about 100 miles from Thousand Lake Mountain southeast to the Colorado River. The upheaval which created it took place some 60 million years ago, and wind and water have since eroded its rocks into a huge variety of forms and textures, as in Capitol Gorge (remaining pictures). Overleaf: the City and County Building in Washington Square, Salt Lake City.

Previous pages: the State Capitol Building in Salt Lake City (overleaf). Far left: heavy storm clouds gather at Inspiration Point, in Bryce Canyon National Park. Bottom right: the sheer canyon walls on the Navajo Loop's Switchback Trail, leading to Wall Street, Bryce Canyon National Park. The strange markings of Checkerboard Mesa (bottom center), in Zion National Park, are the result of weathering along vertical and horizontal planes of weakness in the sandstone. Bottom left: Pectol Pyramid, and (below) the Narrows, in Capitol Gorge (left), Capitol Reef National Park.

Previous pages: well-defined rock
strata exposed (top left) along
the loops of Salt Creek, in the
Needles area of Canyonland's
National Park, and (bottom right)
at Sulphur Creek's Gooseneck.
(Top right) the East Temple, in
Zion Canyon, and (bottom left)
pinnacles of pale rock at Navajo
Loop, Bryce Canyon National Park.
Bryce Canyon (left) is the side
of a plateau, made up of a
complex combination of sediments
– a fine-grained, soft siltstone
and a slightly harder limestone,
interspersed with layers of shale
– laid down when fresh-water
lakes covered the Bryce area
millions of years ago. Water, in
the form of ice, snow and heavy
rains, has since eroded all these
rocks at different rates and to
different effect, to create an
endless variety of formations.
Below: Queen's Garden Trail, and
(bottom) Ponderosa Canyon, both
in Bryce Canyon National Park.

Varying rates of erosion, according to the composition of diffent areas and layers of rock, can be seen clearly (left) at Queen's Garden, Bryce Canyon. The Natural Bridge (below) in Bryce Canyon National Park, was formed by the erosion of the softer, central section of an outcrop of rock, leaving a hole over 50 feet wide and almost twice as high. Bottom left: a wall-like formation on Queen's Garden Trail, and (bottom center) Agua Canyon, both in Bryce Canyon National Park. Bottom right: the serried ranks of Inspiration Point, and (overleaf) Paria View, Bryce Canyon National Park.

The cliffs and towers of Bryce Canyon (these pages) vividly suggest their names. Far left: the view from Rainbow Point, and (below) Balanced Rock. Bottom center left: Gulliver's Castle, in Queen's Garden, and (bottom far left) Queen's Garden Trail. Bottom center right and overleaf: Paria View.

Leached rock pinnacles line the Fairyland Trail (right) and Queen's Garden Trail (below), in Bryce Canyon National Park. Far right: sheer canyon walls on the Navajo Loop's Switchback Trail leading to Wall Street. Facing page: a tall Douglas fir grows in the same area. Overleaf: (left) red Cassidy Arch, Capitol Reef National Park. In Bryce Canyon, slender rock spires crowd Queen's Garden (top right) and Paria View (bottom right).

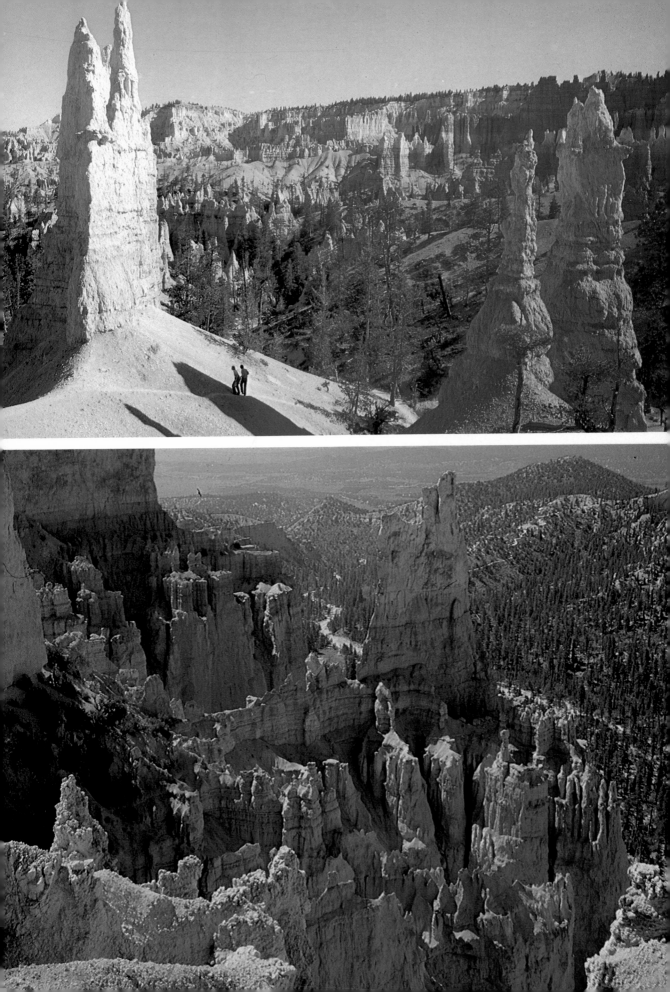

Left: vivid colors at Bryce
Point, and (top) the Wall of
Windows, Bryce Canyon. Above: a
natural bridge on the Navajo Loop
Trail, and (overleaf) delicate
colorings on the Fairyland Trail.

The side canyons of Zion
National Park offer shade
and moisture in which the
leafy aster (right), the
beavertail cactus (bottom
left) and Coulter's
globemallow (bottom right)
all thrive. Below: the
Towers of the Virgin, and
(far right) the Court of the
Patriarchs, in Zion Canyon,
Zion National Park, where
(bottom center and overleaf)
the sun catches the sheer
cliffs of the Watchman.

Top left: East Temple, (center left) Lady Mountain, and (bottom left) the Temples and Towers of the Virgin. Above: the Sentinel, beyond the North Fork of Virgin River, and (center right) Canyon Overlook, Zion Canyon. Center left: golden columbine, and (left) watercress.

Previous pages: Zion Canyon. Top left: the Sentinel in shadow, and (center left) the dark silhouette of the Temples and Towers of the Virgin. Far left: the effects of erosion on crossbedded sandstone. Above: East Temple and (left) Angels Landing, Zion National Park. Golden columbine (top center), and snakeweed (overleaf) flower in Zion National Park.